AN CAWDARN RUDH

AN CAWDARN RUDH
A Companion of Invocations and Charms
For *An Carow Gwyn*

By
Robin Artisson

Illustrations by
Robin Artisson
Stephanie Houser
Jonathan Blackthorn

Layout and Typesetting by
Aidan Grey

© 2018 Robin Artisson. All Rights Reserved. This book or parts thereof may not be reproduced in any form, stored in any retrieval system, or transmitted in any form by any means - electronic, mechanical, photocopy, recording, or otherwise - without prior written permission of the publisher, except as provided by United States of America copyright law.

ISBN-13:
978-1718794030
ISBN-10:
1718794037

BLACK MALKIN PRESS
Bangor, Maine

www.robinartisson.com

Special thanks to Aidan Grey
For his endless patience
And hard work
Putting this book and its big brother
In everyone's hands

CONTAINED HEREIN

Introduction: The Treasures of the Ancient Scrolls...........1

KEY INVOCATIONS

She Who Holds The Plough 9

Spell Of The Thrice-Locked Door 13

Below The Dark Gleaming Land 17

Invocation Of Him From The Four Winds 25

Invocation Of The Ageless Spirit 31

SPELLS AND CHARMS

Conjuration Of The Red Grave 37

Elfhame Prayer 43

Dream Revelation Charm 45

Appeal To The Wort Weird 49

About the Author

Introduction:
The Treasures of the Ancient Scrolls

The sudden noise of a dog barking brought me out of a sound sleep. The room was dark, lit only by the glow of moonlight from outside. *How odd*, I thought. I didn't know any of my neighbors here had dogs. I had been staying in this old farmhouse in New Hampshire for almost 15 months, and this was the first night I had heard a dog.

The barking was deep and loud, like you'd expect a big dog to make. And then it occurred to me: it was *too* loud. It sounded like the dog was right outside of my window. My bedroom was on the second floor of the house; there was no way for a big dog to get on the roof. I don't remember if I tried to move, to go look out of the window and investigate. I lay there, hearing this resounding barking noise over and over, as clear and loud as a bell. For the first minute or so, my mind tried to ignore it, to rationalize it as an ordinary noise anyone might hear living in a rural area. But then another realization began to creep over me; the darkest and strangest of joys leapt up inside me. *It had worked.*

Let's rewind about three or four hours, back to midnight, when I lay down to sleep. I had carried a lit candle to the bedside with me, and spoken aloud an ancient spell to summon a dream oracle. When the Strange Words were all said, I opened my heart and let my feelings gush out like water from a broken dam. I needed guidance, and I had been studying and working with this particular sorcerous formula for a long while. One of its traditional uses was in gaining oracular guidance through dreams, and that's what I needed. Something inside me told me to give it a try that night, and I did.

These powerful words, and their use in conjuring dream oracles (among other things), are described by me in great detail in the work you're holding right now. I decided to include them as part of this collection of invocations and spells because of what happened to me on that night. It was then that I learned the true power those words could unseal within a person's experience.

I lay there listening to the barking of that dog. I couldn't move, but I was relaxed. Something *had* me- but it wasn't threatening or frightening. Moderately disturbing, perhaps, but I felt at peace. The room I was in seemed to be floating separate from the world somehow. I don't know when I stopped hearing the dog, and when the visions arose, but I found myself walking down a dirt road covered with small white stones, through a wooded area.

Up ahead, there was a crossroads. I saw *her* standing there with her back to me. I saw her long red hair. I thought perhaps I'd play a little prank on her, for she didn't seem to notice me no matter how close I got. I figured the crunch of my feet on the gravel would give me away, but it didn't. I had a funny idea: I'd pretend to be an otherworldly being, summoned there by her magic, for I reasoned that she had come to this lonely crossroads in the woods to do some kind of sorcery.

How foolish I was, but at least it was good-natured foolishness. I can't tell you about she and I's subsequent interactions, nor the dream-vision that followed, which showed me things that I very much needed to see. But I *can* say what I was feeling upon waking up.

I knew that there was never any mortal dog outside of my window, and yet I could hear the baritone of its bark echoing in the ears of my memory. I *know* that what I heard was one of the Hounds of the Underworld, a spirit that had been involved in the otherworldly visitation and vision-granting that came to me that night. I was overwhelmed with awe at the power of it all. The hound's spectral sounds left no doubt in me that the *Darkness Formula* had worked. Them below the *dark gleaming land* had heard my request, heard my plea for help, and answered it.

Aside from awe and deep gratitude, I felt something else: I felt a sense of warmth and belonging, a sense that these ancient powers had not only heard me and responded, but considered me a friend, someone they cared for enough to communicate with. I could feel in my bones that I didn't only belong to a community of breathing life in this world, but also to a community of stranger powers and persons in the Unseen. Some part of me was among them. Some part of *all of us* dreams with them, through day and night.

This conclusion is unavoidable; the host of powers which the Darkness Formula opens a gateway to *are* the Ancestresses of us all. We are all products of bloodlines which run back to the dawn of human time, and then to stranger times than that. All of these *red threads* begin in the most sacred and mysterious of places. Surrounding that place are the *Fayerie godmothers* of all humanity, the mothers and grandmothers from Below. They wove the conditions for our lives in the breathing world long ago. They weave the conditions for our lives and deaths still, threading, looping, and knotting from deep within.

They don't always appear as the friendly and sweet grandmother whose house lies *over the river and through the woods* by any means. They dwell close to the roots of things, and their incomprehensible machinations create the story of this world. Sometimes, Fate is a cold and ferocious thing. At other times, it can be pleasant. Fate's intricate patterns are what decide when the *debts of the living* come due. They decide when the highest mountains will be reduced to dust. Sometimes, it is woven that men and women of our world might have needful and blessed visions of *them* from times long forgotten (and even mythical) to modern humans.

How the Darkness Formula's dream oracle worked for me on that night might bear little resemblance to how it works for you. I only know that it *works*, powerfully so. If you have the need, and the proper insight and reverence, it will unseal a vision for you.

This book, *An Cawdarn Rudh*, or The Red Cauldron, is a collection of nine spells and charms that come from the most ancient source of historical sorcerous workings that we have: the *Papyri Graecae Magicae*. Each one of them is a key which potentially opens a gateway to another time and another world. Each one of them barely survived a widespread purge of books and scrolls which took place in the third century of the Common Era, when the insurgent Christian Church gained enough power to order the wholesale destruction of magical and sorcerous texts across the dying Roman Empire.

I wrote this book so that those who had begun studying and using my book *An Carow Gwyn* would have access to further potent historical workings, that they might increase the range and power of their sorcerous and spiritual practices. Those who own *An Carow Gwyn* already understand what a *Key Invocation* is and how it is used. *An Carow Gwyn* gave five Key Invocations. This book contains five more, to be used in precisely the same manner as the first five, and with the same grave warnings.

This book also contains four other workings: a charm for gaining dream revelations from the Ancient White One or one of his serving-spirits, a spell for protection, a very powerful work of primordial necromancy, and an alternate *Herb Swaying Charm*, all of them drawn from the ancient source material, and proven through my own experience to be highly effective. This book contains all the guidance needed to bring these nine workings to life within the framework of sorcery outlined in *An Carow Gwyn*. These are precious gemstones from within the treasure-hoard of the surviving ancient scrolls. They have helped me immeasurably for many years, and I hope they will help you, too.

Those who do not have access to *An Carow Gwyn* might still be able to get some use or insight from the invocations, spells and charms given here. Only study, effort, and time would tell, but I think an able or experienced occultist could (so long as they have a genuine sense of reverence) find a way to adapt these workings to another framework or metaphysical system. The powers behind these workings are real, and far more intelligent than we. They know when a man or woman is trying to reach them.

When you set out to perform one of these workings, remember it is important that the sounds of the "Strange Words" be pronounced properly. The *Semoferas* words (such as those given at the beginning of the *Appeal to the Wort Weird*) can be pronounced as you wish; but the words that I give pronunciations for should be pronounced just as indicated. It is acceptable to write out the phonetic pronunciations and have them with you, to read aloud when you do the work, or to read directly from this book. So long as you are reading by natural light, all is well. Few people can really commit the lengthier Strange Word sequences and their pronunciations to memory.

The vowel sound **AI**, which appears in some of the Strange words in this book (as well as within *An Carow Gwyn*) can be pronounced "ay", or like the English word "eye." In *An Carow Gwyn*, I chose to express that sound as "eye", and in this book, I express it as "ay." Both are correct and interchangeable with one another; use whichever sounds more appealing to you, whether in this work or in the invocations given in *An Carow Gwyn*.

The sorcerous life-way is supported by real Otherworldly powers. They live, they know us, and they relate to us, whether we are aware of their subtle presences or not. To become more aware of them, to be able to show them respect and reverence, and to receive their blessings (or their warnings): this is a joy and wonder which is rare these days. *An Carow Gwyn* showed how to open many traditional doorways to the strange depths of this world. *An Cawdarn Rudh* now gives nine more. May you have good luck in all of your workings, and may you know the friendship of the *Good Folk* in the Unseen.

Robin Artisson
May 2018

KEY INVOCATIONS

SHE WHO HOLDS THE PLOUGH

To utilize this potent invocation of petition, you must be able to see the northern stars- chiefly the constellation of Ursa Major, which was called the Great Bear by the ancients of Southern Europe, and The Wain by those of the North. It was called The Plough in Britain and Ireland. The region of the night sky containing the constellations Ursa Major and Draco was the region of the "Undying Stars" or the "Stars That Never Set", representing not only the immortal or eternal aspect of all things and beings, but the Unseen World itself and its ruling powers and ageless daimons. The Seven-Starred Plough, or Ursa Major, points towards the Pole Star, the unmoving "nail of the sky" or navel of the sky around which all the stars rotate, representing the ancient, Titanic feminine force of cosmic Fate and Necessity: the Fateful hand that directs the great cycles of the living world. It also acts as a sign-post to the soul country, the primordial land or the spiritual homeland of humanity and all life.

Sit or stand facing the Northern Stars, perform your Breaching charm and then (while gazing upon them) say:

> "Great Plough which rides in the black meadow of the stars, which moves on ancient tracks through the endless darkness, you Mighty Weaver who yet rules over the stars and the plough, who makes the sky turn and the blossom come to branch; who makes the snow fall and the wombs of women fill with souls from the dark waters below; who ordains that burial grounds fill with pale corpses and the final exhalation of hopes: you are the Spinner of Fate, the one who binds Necessity fast around every shape in the world. I appeal to you, Dark and Bright One, imploring you and supplicating you that you will (here describe your need), because I call upon you with the holy names at which your spirit rejoices, ancient names you will never ignore:
>
> **BRIMÔ:** You who overcomes all Earthly powers, bringing them to their end, fast-riding Huntress!
>
> **BAUBÔ LAUMORI AUMÔR AMÔR AMÔRES IÊA**: You who sends arrows swift and lethal, killing the deer that you chase;

AMAMAMAR APHROUMATHAMA: Queen of the world entire, Queen of the Elfin country, and granter of wishes;

AMAMA: You whose bed is good and restful, Queen of Fayerie Elfhame, who sees all from the bent branches of trees and the dark corners of houses, who wanders through the night, who slays men, who summons men at your will, and who seduces men;

LICHRISSA PHAESSA: You who flies through the air leading the Host of Spirits as seasons turn, who keeps the homes of the generous free from want, Queen with her seven serving women, who commands the song and the dance, whose eye sees all things clandestinely, whose beauty is rare and delicate, whose sovereign will knows no compromise, who bends not, O Damnameneia!

BREXERIKANDARA: You who tears men to pieces and soaks them in a cauldron, Secret and Exalted One, Taurine, whose beauty and soul is ineffable, whose body is luminous, armed with the sharp arrows of deadly Fate."

(Again speak here what you need or desire.)

* * *

Pronunciation of the Strange Words used in this invocation:

bree-moh

boe-boe loh-mah-ree oh-more ah-more ah-more-ess ee-ay-ah

ah-mah-mah-mar ah-proo-mah-tah-mah

ah-mah-mah

lee-kree-sah pah-ess-ah

breks-eh-ree-khan-dar-ah

"khan" is pronounced like the title "khan" as in "Genghis Khan."

SPELL OF THE THRICE-LOCKED DOOR

This invocation of petition is to be performed during the waning moon. Its power is increased if you can gaze upon the moon from outdoors, or at least through a window, while performing your rite, but this is not strictly necessary. You will need a mirror of some kind to perform this key invocation. Perform your Breaching charm, and then say:

> "Hail to you in the holy light of the moon, the Queen of Spirits, ruler of Annwn, who strikes with rays of ghostly light in the darkness. Hail, Luminous One who turns and appears out of the darkness to confound the aimless men and women of this world. I call upon you now, and may you hear my words, for the powers of Fate and Destiny are subject to you, all of them your serving women. Lady thrice-bound, set yourself free, for the Fates will spin out their threads for you.
>
> Assent to me, I beg of you Blessed One, and do not raise your hand against me, nor send the arrows of the Fateful Host against me; do not be angered by my appeals. Think kindly of me, who wanders in this vast and dark world, yearning for the peace of your blessed land, the ancestral home of all souls in the deep. Great Elven Queen who leads hounds in the hunt, lend aid to me with (*speak your need or desire here.*)
>
> For I know your beauty and your greatness, and the tales told of you; I am devoted to you, one who makes offerings and speaks prayers to you in the dark, and in the lonely places of the world; I bear witness to your great name, Maiden of Maidens. Let no power or person escape my will or resist the fulfillment of my desire; aid me with (*speak your desire here again.*)
>
> Now I call to you on this potent night, in which your light is the last to fade away; in which the hound opens, but closes not its mouth; in which the sealed spaces of the Underworld are opened, and whence comes the Lord of baying hounds, with thunder following.

Bestir yourself, Gwynnevar, who nurses even the sun, who protects the dead of this world; you I implore, Maiden, by your light which fills the night, you I entreat, the cunning one, swiftly and invisibly moving, Healer, you who have greatest forethought, fearless, crimson, darkness, **BRIMÔ**, undying, who hears all pleas, Lady of the Meadow, crowned with the golden flowers of spring, worshiped in Elder Times, shining over the sea, eldritch, pale, beautiful, who reveals all, whose arrows cannot miss their mark, self-generating, Leader of the Spirit-Host, who knows many sorrows, who can take the shape of a wolf.

You are hated by the world of unwise men, you are the destroyer, grim-eyed, loud-screaming, O Nethermost One, known to the secret heart of the wide world, running as a hound, Spinner of Fate, All-Giver, eternal, helper of man, Lady Bright, Queen of Fayerie, holy, benign, deathless, whose locks are glossy; you are the one who is in bloom, bright-faced, who presides over the birth of children, wise, malevolent when thy will turns, shooter of arrows, Maiden; I know that you are most clever, and can deliver all from fear.

Hear me: **EÔ PHORBA BRIMÔ SACHMI NEBOUTO SOUALÊTH** for I know a secret sign of yours: the sandal you wear upon your foot, and I know of your key. I have breached the seal of the Underworld; I have parted the hedge which guards the way to Annwn, and my words I send into darkness, where you hear all things. Gaze into my mirror here, the most ancient of love charms, and cast any dark light from your eyes and help me, who calls out to you. Mare, Maiden, Great Serpent, Lamp, Flash of Lightning, Star, Doe, Cat, She-Wolf, **AÊÔ ÊÊ**.

A sieve, an old utensil, is your symbol, and one morsel of flesh, a piece of coral, the blood of a dove, a hoof, the hair of a virgin cow, the seed of the Terrifying One, fire from a ray of the sun, the foot of a colt, spindle tree, youthful love, a fire bow, a grey-eyed woman's body with her legs outspread, a vagina: all of these are the ancient signs of your power.

By all the forces bound in this world by Fate- the radiant sun, the pale moon that glows in murky night, eternity and wearisome time, the pole around which the stars turn, the oceans that caress the shores and stones, the green hedges and forests, the living above and the dead below- turn your kind help towards me, for I know your signs and secret things. Here I speak of them further: I speak of the bronze sandal of you who rule in the Great Darkness below; I speak of your wreath, your key, your wand, your wheel, the Black Dog, your Thrice-Locked Door, your burning hearth, your shadow, depth, fire, you who are the Governess of the powers of Annwn.

Hear me and help me; let my desires and my needs come to pass, for I know your good and great names by which the sky is filled with light, and earth drinks dew and becomes pregnant; from these names, the entire world increases and declines:

EUPHORBA PHORBA PHORBOREOU PHORBA PHORBOR PHORBOR PHORBOR BORBORPHA ÊRPHOR PHORBAIÔ PHORBOR PHORBOR BOROPH PHORPHOR BORPHORBOR AÔ IÔÊ PHORBORPHOR EUPHOR BOPHOR EUOIEÔ PHÔTH IÔPHÔTH IÔPHÔTH PHÔTHIÔPH AÔÔÔTHO ÔAI IÔ EÔÔIÔ HAHAHA EE ÊÊ IOYY ÔÔÔ OYYYY AEÊIOUÔ YYY, Mistress of the World Entire, aid me in attaining what I have entreated you for this night."

* * *

Pronunciation of the Strange Words used in this invocation:

bree-moh

ee-oh par-bah bree-moh sock-mee neh-boo-tah soo-ah-late

ah-ay-oh ay-ay

yew-par-bah par-bah par-bar-eh-oo par-bah par-bar par-bar par-bar bar-bar-pah air-par par-bay-oh par-bar par-bar bah-rop par-par bar-par-bar ah-oh ee-oh-ay par-bar-par yew-par bah-par yew-oy-eh-oh poat ee-oh-poat ee-oh-poat poe-tee-ope ah-ohhhhhh-tah oh-ay ee-oh eh-ohhh-ee-oh ah-ah-ah (*make these three sounds short and raspy*) ehhh ayyyy ee-ah-ooo ohhhh ah-oooo ahh-ehh-ayy-eee-ooo-ohh oooo

15

BELOW THE DARK GLEAMING LAND

The following Key Invocation is a special sequence of ten powerful words, which can be used for several different sorcerous and spiritual operations. These ten words are a variant form of what historians call the *Ephesia Grammata*, or the "Ephesian Letters." The original Ephesian Letters were said to be carved upon the famed primal image of Artemis which stood in the Temple of Ephesus. These words were believed to have been revealed to human beings by a group of spirits who were powerful in sorcery and artifice and who served the Earth Mother or the Earth Indweller; later they were believed to be a special group of her offspring. They may have reflected a dim memory of a primordial group of culture-creating sorcerers. They were called the *Dactyls*.

This link between Artemis and these words, and the link between Artemis/Diana and the Fayerie Queen of the Ancient Fayerie Faith, is profound on many levels. The association of these words (along with Artemis) and the sorcery-empowering Queen of the Underworld in the ancient magical scrolls, is likewise historically clear. I call this variation of the Ephesian Letters the *Darkness Formula* for reasons I shall give shortly.

The Darkness Formula can be used as a Key Invocation, and this will likely be its main usage for people engaging this sorcerous system. Historically, it was also used for death aversion, rescue from spiritual danger, for invoking a potent dream oracle, and it could be used to create lots utilized in divination. I will begin by giving the full formula, along with very detailed instructions for the proper pronunciation of all ten words. It is essential that those who will utilize this formula completely memorize the words and sounds, and be able to say them easily from memory.

This memorization is not of the ordinary kind; one should *internalize* these words to a deep degree. Begin by saying them aloud (though with a soft voice) until one can simply repeat them silently within one's mind. Then continue to repeat them- for days or weeks if one must- until they can spontaneously spring from the tongue at a moment's need. After one has internalize the Darkness Formula in such a way, they should *never* be spoken aloud unless it is during a sorcerous or spiritual working.

The words are:

ASKEI KATASKEI ERÔN OREÔN
IÔR MEGA SAMNYÊR BAUI
PHOBANTIA SEMNÊ

And they are pronounced as follows:

ASKEI: ah-skay

KATASKEI: kuh-tah-skay

ERÔN: eh-rown (rown rhymes with "grown")

OREÔN: ah-reh-own (the "eh" in "reh" sounds like the "e" in the name "Ed.")

IÔR: ee-yore

MEGA: meh-gah

SAMNYÊR: sahm-new-air (the "sahm" rhymes with the name "Tom.")

BAUI: bow-ee (the "bow" here is like the "bow" in "bow and arrow.")

PHOBANTIA: pah-bahn-tee-uh (the "bahn" here sounds like the "bon" in "bond.")

SEMNÊ: sem-nay

* * *

Unlike many of the Strange Words used in the historical sources, these words have understandable meanings. This does not interrupt the deep impact they have on the mind and soul when said under the proper ritual conditions. To comprehend their meaning endows us with an appreciation of the depth of their origins and the powerful spirit-persons they can connect us with. For these words create a direct portal or gateway between our own souls and a host of Fateful powers- the Fate-Women themselves- who surround the Underworld Queen.

This formula gains the attentions of the Queen Below and her serving-women, the feminine powers who have command over birth, life, fertility, and death, who were reverenced all over Europe in many forms: they were called the Disir, the Good Mothers, the Fayerie Godmothers, the Furies, the Fates, the Spinners, the Norns, and so forth.

The first eight words of the formula translate into something like the following:

> *"Below the shadowy mountains, in the dark gleaming land, IOR! The Great Loud-Sounding (or singing) One! BAUI!*

"IOR" represents an ecstatic shout. "BAUI" is an imitative word intending to simulate the sound of hounds or dogs barking. The final two words of the formula- PHOBANTIA SEMNÊ- is an epithet for the Great Queen herself, which translates as *"Awe-inspiring, Terrifying One."*

There is no doubt in my mind that this formula is invoking the historical presence (and historical memory) of female-centered sorcerous groups that were devoted to the Queen of Spirits and the feminine-appearing Fateful spirit-powers that surround her, whom they interacted with in the course of Fate-related witchery and other kinds of dark sorcerous works.

The word SAMNYÊR, which means "loud-sounding", is a reference to ecstatic chanting and shouting, the projection of sorcerous spells and magical sounds utilized by these sorceresses. This connects to the "BAUI" or the baying of the spirit-hounds: the Underworldly hounds of Annwn. These ancient witches were the *barking bitches* of the Underworld with their chants and sorcerous songs. "The Loud Sounding One" is not just an able epithet for the Queen of Sorcery herself, but for her human followers, too.

The deep connection between dogs and hounds revealed here is another example of consistently emerging folkloric symbol-language, as we see even in our later Fayerie Tales wherein the Fayerie Queen is depicted in the company of canine beings. Hekate- herself associated with the Fayerie Queen and tutelary spirit of witches in Europe's pre-modern period- is likewise historically associated with dogs. The source-scroll for the Darkness Formula is clearly *Hekatean* in its metaphysical associations. The first word of the sequence- Askei- means *shadowless*, which poetically expresses complete darkness because there is no light to cast shadows.

* * *

To utilize the Darkness Formula as a Key Invocation, you perform a Breaching charm, and then say the first eight words three times, and the final two words once. Then follows a phrase to be stated in which you assert your familiarity with the mysteries of the Underworld, and then you make your request for whatever desire or need you have. This work is best done at night, but if you work during the day, it is best to be in direct contact with the earth itself. The entire petition-invocation is given here, as it should be said:

> "ASKEI KATASKEI ERÔN OREÔN
> IÔR MEGA SAMNYÊR BAUI;
> ASKEI KATASKEI ERÔN OREÔN
> IÔR MEGA SAMNYÊR BAUI;
> ASKEI KATASKEI ERÔN OREÔN
> IÔR MEGA SAMNYÊR BAUI;
> PHOBANTIA SEMNÊ!
>
> I have been initiated; I have gone down
> Into the dark caverns of the Underworld,
> Where the Ancient and Cunning Ones,
> Supreme in artifice, carry out their works.
> I saw many things below the dark land:
> I saw the virgin, the bitch, and all the rest."

(Here state your need or desire.)

The ancient scroll indicates that if these words are said at a Crossroads, they have great power- and a warning is given that "She" may appear there at the recitation. This should not be taken to mean that the Queen of the Underworld or her representative serving-spirits are malicious by any means; but their grim majesty and sheer Otherworldly power can carry with it many degrees of awe, terror, and a potential hard impact upon the human mind and soul.

To carry out this Key Invocation at a crossroads (which means either a place where two roads cross, creating four roads, or a place where a single road forks, creating three roads) is the most powerful stage for this work. To use one of the Crossways signs or a Portal knot places you symbolically (and thus metaphysically *actually*) at a Crossroads. This invocation is thus very accessible in many places. But it must be respected. It can never be used in anything other than a reverential and careful manner. The Dark Mothers hear these words when they are properly pronounced and especially when said in the proper special places or under extraordinary conditions. They become aware of the person or persons saying them, and the place they are said.

The source of this invocation also mentions that it can be used as a powerful method of obtaining a dream oracle. As I revealed earlier in this work, I know this to be true from a potent personal experience. The ancient scroll's instructions are written as follows: "If you say (these words) late at night, and follow them with matters you wish to know about, it will be revealed to you in your sleep."

If you wish to gain a dream-oracle from the Darkness Formula, go to bed a little later than usual, and take a candle or lantern with you. Purify yourself with some traditional method, then sit in bed with your lit candle, and focus on the sensation of your body. When calm, say the entire formula just as it is given above for use as a key invocation, and when you reach the point where you would ask for help with a need or desire, speak honestly and candidly about the problem that is troubling you, or the thing you wish the dream to reveal to you. You can ask for guidance, advice, or visions of how the future for a certain situation will play out.

Do not be sparing with details, and don't be shy. Feel free to speak your whole heart, gush about your feelings, your fears, and your concerns regarding your situation. There is no one around to judge you on what you say, and the powers that will be listening to you aren't judgmental about these things. If you become emotional, that's all the better: it will increase your openness to what is going to arise in the night. Then, extinguish your candle and go to sleep, watching for your dream.

My own experiences of the Darkness Formula were so profound, that it swiftly became a cornerstone not only of my sorcerous practice, but my spiritual life. When giving offerings to the Fate-women and the Fayerie Godmothers, these internalized sacred words have never failed to act as a potent bridge to their spirits.

* * *

The last traditional uses of this formula that I wish to expand upon, is regarding its use as a protective charm and death aversion charm. If you should ever find yourself in a deep trance state, or in a shimmering state born from lucid dreaming (as discussed in *An Carow Gwyn*), or in any situation of shimmering or out-of-body experience in which you feel threatened by a hostile spirit-being, the Darkness Formula can preserve you. Simply say the words (all ten of them in their simple sequence, you need not repeat the first eight three times) and, if you can, enclose your two thumbs inside of your hands. Then say **"I am the Queen of the Great Earth, the one holding her thumbs, and not even one evil can befall her!"**

It doesn't matter what sex you are; men can identify with the "Queen of the Great Earth" sorcerously and symbolically simply through using these words. Many of those who use the Darkness Formula as a Key Invocation are already using words to identify as a person who has been "initiated"- and whether or not that is true, it symbolically and metaphysically *becomes true* through using these words in the ritual moment.

If your first attempt to ward off the threatening power doesn't work, you should seize your right heel with either of your hands, and say "**Queen of the Great Earth! Virgin! Bitch! Serpent! Wreathe! Key! Herald's Staff! Golden shoe of the Lady of Elfhame!**" And then it is said that you will be left alone; the menacing spirit will be averted. These efforts at spirit-aversion will also work for you beyond the boundaries of this life: if, in the transitional journey beyond your own death, you fall foul of menacing or challenging spirits, these words can preserve you then, too. This is another reason why it is good to internalize this formula so well; if it becomes a deep part of your being in life, you will take it with you onto the ghost-roads and beyond.

If, during your life, you are given bad news about your approaching death- whether from a doctor, or another source, the Darkness Formula can potentially drive away the hungry Fates that will be circling you, or at least make them relax their fierceness enough to temporarily spare you over. The ancient scroll says "If you are led away to death, say the words (the Darkness Formula as you would say it if using it as a Key invocation) while scattering sesame seeds from your hand, and it will save you."

I believe that any small or oily seed can be used in this attempt.

INVOCATION OF HIM FROM THE FOUR WINDS

This invocation is traditionally timed to coincide with the rising sun, though I believe it could be performed towards a rising moon as well. "Rising" doesn't have to indicate the sun (or the moon) just as it appears over the horizon, though that would be a potent time for performing this invocation; it can refer to the sun or moon at any early point during the course of their rising, before they obtain too high of a position in the sky. Perform your Breaching charm, and then say:

> "Come to me Ancient White One, you whose dwelling is within the four winds, you the ruler and protector of the world entire, who breathed the spirit of life into men and women, who breathed the spirit of life into the beasts of the forest and the field, into the birds that fly above, and into the fish that move in the cold depths below. The boughs of trees shake with your soul-giving breath. The mighty storms shout with your voice. Your true name is hidden and unspeakable; it cannot be uttered by the human mouth; the spirits of dark Annwn and all invisible regions are terrified when that name resounds.
>
> Yours is the sun shrouded in white mist, **ARNEBOUAT BOLLOCH BARBARICH B BAALSAMÊN PTIDAIOY ARNEBOUAT**;
>
> Yours is the moon in darkest night, **ARSENPENPRÔOUTH BARBARAIÔNE OSRAR MEMPSECHEI**;
>
> The sun and moon are thy unwearied eyes, which shine in the depths of the eyes of men and women: they are the eyes of You for whom the broad sky is head, for whom the wind is body, for whom the earth is hunting ground, for whom the whole world is flowing life, you the Wild and Blessed One. You move over the ocean, making waves to crest with white, bringing its great bounty to all who come to its shores seeking food. Yours is the eternal road of the sky, in which your name of Seven Sounds creates a harmony by which great powers seen and unseen utter their voices, all within the twenty-eight secret shapes of the moon:

SAR APHARA APHARA I ABRAARM ARAPHA ABRAACH PERTAÔMÊCH AKMÊCH IAÔ OYE Ê IAÔ OYE EIOY AEÔ EÊOY IAÔ.

Yours are the benevolent fluxes and motions of the distant stars that bring fortune onto men and women; numbered within your Host are the spirits that hunt and kill, alongside wealful spirits and kindly Fates by which men and women receive wealth, good old age, good children, good luck, good death, and good burial. You, Lord of Life, Chieftain over the Winds and the Earth and all the living things within them, your justice is impossible to evade. It is your name the spirits who inspire men to song all sing.

Ê Ô CHÔ CHOUCH NOUN NAUNI AMOUN AMAUNI: you possess the truth that does not perish nor lie. Your world-moving spirit and your favors rest upon the good. Come into my mind and my understanding for all the days of my life, and grant me all the desires of my soul.

For I am within you, and you within me; whatever I say using the holy wind of my body, that must happen, for I have your name as a spell of power within my heart. No flesh, whatever shall move it, will overcome me; no spirit will stand against me, neither hungry power nor any wicked spirit from Annwn, because of your name which I have in my soul and which I invoke. Be with me always for my great luck and thriving, a protective spirit dwelling with me; you are immune to magic, so give me health that no magic may harm, alongside well-being, prosperity, triumph over any challenges, power, and appeal to those I desire. Restrain the evil eyes and sorceries of those who hate me, whether spirit, man, or woman, and give me charm in everything I set out to do.

ANOCH AIEPHE SAKTIETÊ BIBIOU BIBIOU SPHÊ SPHÊ NOUSI NOUSI SEÊE SEÊE SIETHÔ SIETHÔ OUN CHOUNTIAI SEMBI IMENOUAI BAINPHNOUN PHNOUTH TOUCHAR SOUCHAR SABACHAR ANA of the Lordly Spirit **IEOU ION EON THÔTHÔ OUTHRO THRÔRESE ERIÔPÔ IYÊ AÊ IAÔAI AEÊIOYÔ AEÊIOYÔ ÊOCH MANEBI CHYCHIÔ ALARAÔ KOL KOL KAATÔN KOLKANTHÔ BALALACH ABLALACH**

OTHERCHENTHE BOULÔCH BOULÔCH OSERCHNTHE MENTHEI, for I have received the power of the Lord of the Host of Spirits, **IAÔ ABLANATHANALBA SIABRATHILAÔ LAMPSTÊR IÊI ÔÔ,** Great One, accomplish this, Lord **PERTAÔMÊCH CHACHMÊCH IAÔ OYÊE IEOU AÊÔ EÊOY IAÔ.**"

Face the rising sun (or moon), stretch your right and left arms both to your left, and intone the sound **AHHHHH**.

Turn and face north, put forward only your right fist, and intone the sound **EHHHHHH**.

Then turn to face west, put both hands out in front of you, and intone the sound **AYYYYY**.

Turn to face south, put both hands on your stomach, and intone the sound **EEEEEEE**.

Face east again. Crouch down or bend down to the earth, placing your hands on your toes or upon the earth, and intone the sound **AWWWWW**.

Stand, look into the air above you, place your right hand over your heart and intone the sound **OOOOOO**.

Now look directly up into the sky, with your hands touching either side of your head, and intone the sound **OHHHHH**.

Then say:

> "I call upon you, Master within the Great Wind that fills the world, Ancient One, Lasting One, who moves all things, who binds all things, strange one whom none can understand, whom all the spirits revere, whose name they dare not utter. Fill with power from your exhalation, Master of the Pole Star, he (or she) who is here below you, and accomplish for me (*say your need here.*)

* * *

Pronunciation of the Strange Words used in this invocation:

ar-neh-boo-aht bah-lock bar-bar-eek buh ball-sah-main p'tee-day-oo ar-neh-boo-aht

ar-sen-pen-pro-oot bar-bar-ay-own-eh ahs-rar memp-seh-kay

sar ah-para ah-para ee abra-arm ah-rah-pah abra-ock per-tah-oh-make ock-make ee-ah-oh oo-eh ay ee-ah-oh oo-eh ay-oo ah-eh-oh eh-ay-oo ee-ah-oh

ay oh koh kook noon known-ee ah-moon ah-moan-ee

ah-nock ay-ep-eh sock-tee-eh-tay bee-bee-oo bee-bee-oo spay spay noo-see noo-see seh-ay-eh seh-ay-eh see-eh-toe see-eh-toe oon koon-tee-ay sem-bee ee-men-oo-ay bain-puh-noon puh-noo't too-kar soo-kar sah-bah-kar ah-nah … ee-eh-oo ee-ahn eh-ahn toe-toe oo-trah troar-eh-seh eh-ree-oh-poh ee-oo-ay ah-ay ee-ah-oh-ay ah-eh-ay-ee-ah-oo-oh ah-eh-ay-ee-ah-oo-oh ay-ock mah-neb-ee koo-kee-oh ah-lah-rah-oh kall kall kah-ah-tone kall-kan-toe bah-lah-lock ah-blah-lock otter-ken-teh boo-loak boo-loak ah-serken-teh men-tay … ee-ah-oh ah-blah-not-en-all-bah see-ah-brah-tee-lah-oh lahmp-stair ee-ay-ee oh-oh … per-tah-oh-make cock-make ee-ah-oh oo-ay-eh ee-eh-oo ah-ay-oh eh-ay-oo ee-ah-oh

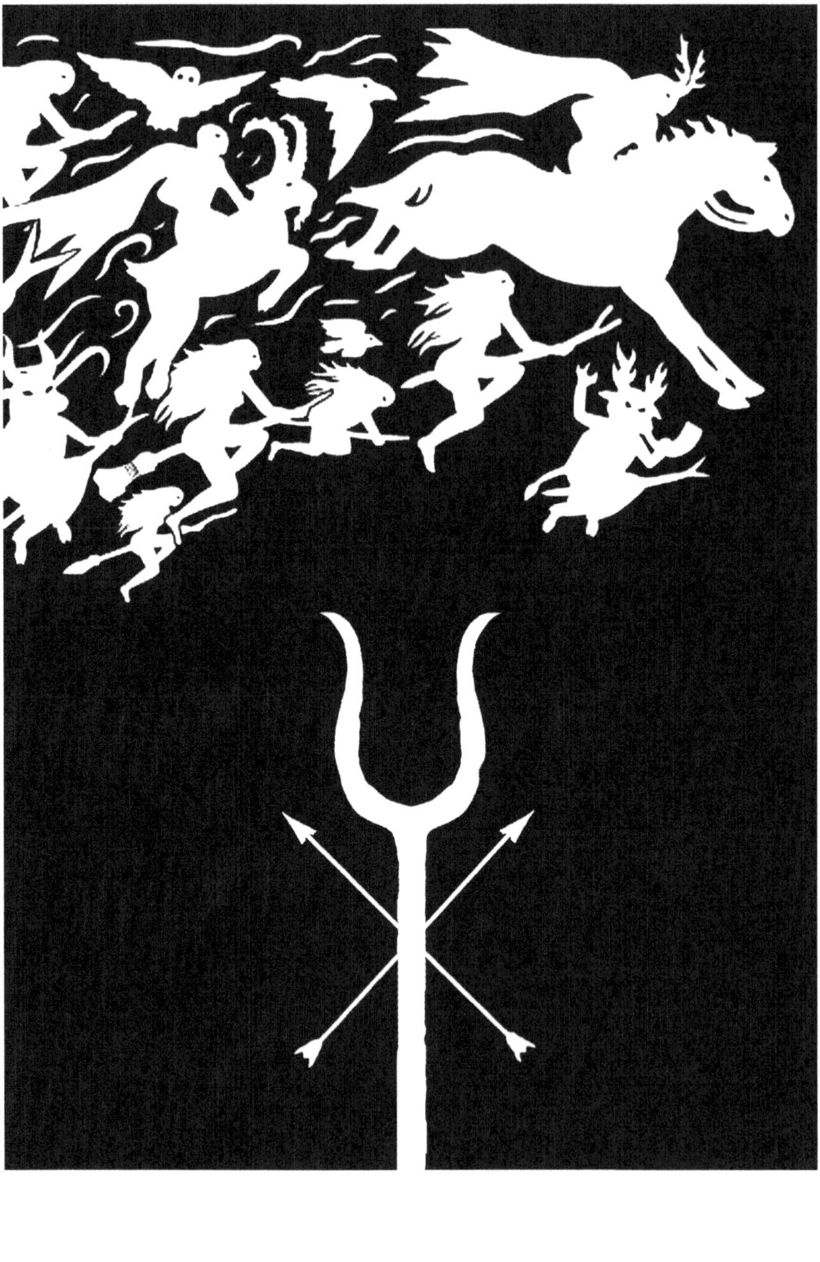

INVOCATION OF THE AGELESS SPIRIT

"I call to you Gwyn, the Sacred one, the White one, the Pure one, the Blessed one, Master of the ages of the world. Come to me Forefather, who filled the sky with winds, who with secret strength joined and separated the ancient powers and shaped the Land and Sky.

Give heed, you spirits within the air, the earth, and the sea to my words here, for I am wise concerning the hidden powers and them who weave Fate. Let each of my words become a fiery dart or a flying arrow, because I am a man (or woman) who contains the breath soul of the Great Spirit of the Winds; I am shaped of breath, dew, and earth.

Let the sky open and the winds accept my words: Hear me, Gwyn ap Nudd, Master of the Hunt, Father of the world, I call upon you with your name:

AÔ EY ÊOI AIOÊ YEÔA OUORZARA LAMANTHATHRÊ KANTHIOPER GARPSARTHRÊ MENLARDAPA KENTHÊR DRYOMEN THRANDRÊTHRÊ IABE ZELANTHI BER ZATHRÊ ZAKENTI BIOLLITHRÊ AÊÔ OYÔ ÊÔ OÔ RAMIATHA AÊÔ ÔYÔ OYÔ ÔAYÔ:
You who bear the root power of life.

Yours is the holy and terrible Name feared and adored by all spirits; protect me (NN) from every excess of power, from every wicked spirit, and from every deed of violence. Yes, do this you who rides at the head of the arrow-sending host, stronger than all:

IALDAZAÔ BLATHAM MACHÔR PHRIX AÊ KEÔPH EÊA DYMEÔ PHERPHRITHÔ IACHTHÔ PSYCHEÔ PHIRITHMEÔ RÔSERÔTH THAMASTRAPHATI RIMPSAÔCH IALTHE MEACHI ARBATHANÔPS

Enlivener of the world, shaper of the world, Great Huntsman, **MARMARIÔ IAÔ**.

I have spoken of your power which cannot be cast down, you who have given life to so many beings. The dreadful troop of the Sheevra follows you through the bright and dark sky; they know your wisdom and your eternity: **IEOYÊOÊ IAÊAIÊÓÊYOEI.**

I call upon your great name, which secretly moves from the sky to the depths of the earth; preserve me and favor me, for you are always good to your own:

ATHÊZE PHÔI AAA DAIAGTHI THÊOBIS PHIATH THAMBRAMI ABRAÔTH CHTHOLCHIL THOE OELCHÔTH THIOÔÊMCH CHOOMCH SAÊSI ISACHCHOÊ IEROUTHRA OOOOO AIÔAI

I call upon you, whose windy breath moves the whole world, whose light fills the whole world:

IAÔ AIÊ IÔÊ ÔIÊ ÔIÊ IÊ AIÔAI AI OYÔ AÔÊ ÊEI IEÔ ÊYÔ AÊI AÔ AÔA AEÊI YÔ EIÊ AÊÔ IEY AEÊ IAIA IAÔ EY AEY IAÊ EI AAA III ÊÊÊ IÔ IÔÊ IAÔ for thy blessing, Lord."

(This invocation confers a general protection and blessing upon all who say it, or upon those it is said for. If you have a further need, here you say "Fulfill for me this need/deed XX", etc.)

* * *

Pronunciation of the Strange Words used in this invocation:

Ah-oh yew ay-oy ay-ah-ay oo-eh-oh-ah oo-ar-zah-rah lah-mahn-tah-tray khan-tee-ahp-er garp-sar-tray men-lar-dah-pah ken-tayer droo-ah-men tron-dray-tray ee-ah-buh zell-ahn-tee ber zah-tray zah-ken-tee bee-ah-lee-tray ah-ay-oh oo-oh ay-oh ah-oh rah-mee-ah-tah ah-ay-oh oh-oo-oh ah-oo-oh oh-ow-oh

ee-all-dah-zah-oh blah-tom mah-core preeks ah-ay keh-ope eh-ay-ah doo-meh-oh per-pree-toe ee-yock-toe soo-keh-oh peer-eet-meh-oh roe-ser-roat tom-ah-struh-pah-tee reemp-sah-oak ee-all-tuh meh-ock-ee ar-buh-tahn-opes

mar-mar-ee-oh ee-ah-oh

ee-eh-oo-ay-ah-ay ee-ah-ay-eye-ay-oh-ay-oo-ah-ay

ah-tay-zeh poe-ee ahhhhhhh day-ahg-tee tay-ob-iss pee-ot tom-brom-ee ah-brah-oat kuh-tall-kill tah-eh ah-ell-coat tee-ah-oh-aim'k kah-ahm'k sah-ay-see ee-sah-kuh-kah-ay ee-eh-roo-trah ahhhhhh ay-oh-ay

ee-ah-oh eye-ay ee-oh-ay oh-ee-ay oh-ee-ay ee-ay ay-oh-ay ay oo-oh ah-oh-ay ay-ay ee-eh-oh ay-oo-oh ah-ay-ee ah-oh ah-oh-ah ah-eh-ay-ee oo-oh eh-ee-ay ah-ay-oh ee-eh-oo ah-eh-ay ee-ay-ah ee-ah-oh oo- ah-oo ee-ah-ay ay ahhhhh eeeee ayyyyyy ee-oh ee-oh-ay ee-ah-oh

SPELLS *And* CHARMS

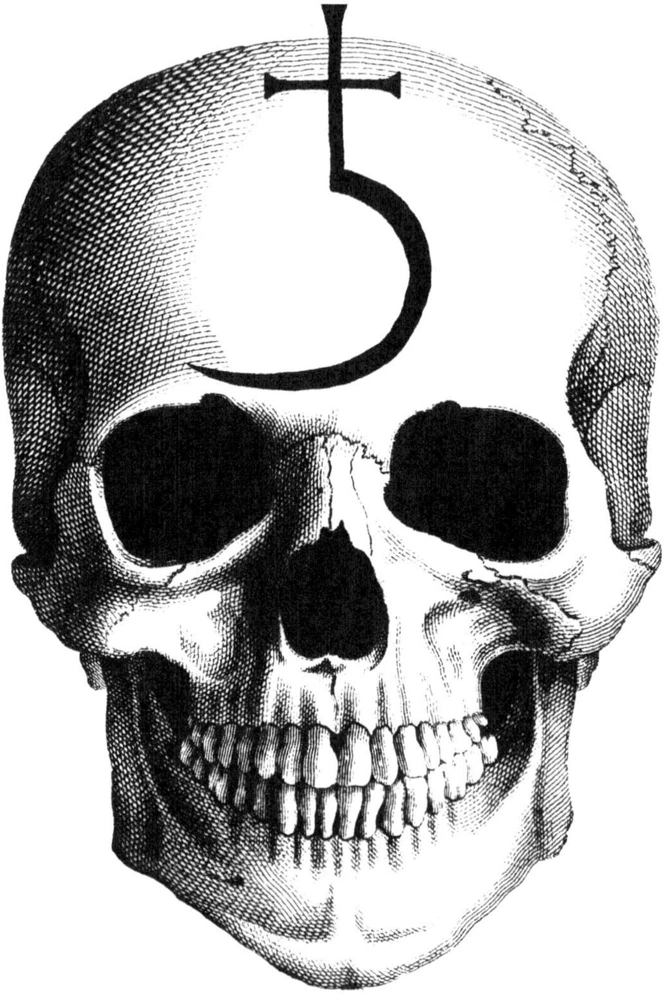

CONJURATION OF THE RED GRAVE

This ancient spell was historically assayed to cause a person to become attracted to another, an aggressive *Venusian-Saturnian* necromantic working which called upon the souls of dead men or women to empower this lust-compulsion. There are "red" elements to this Saturnian work, for the dead who were appealed to (and sometimes compelled) for their help were those who had died violently *and* recently- those who had died shortly before the spell was performed. There is a traditional connection, in the sorcery of the very old times, between the souls of the violently slain and all manner of sorcerous feats, but *especially* amatory workings and workings of vengeance.

This spell can be used for any goal one may have, but it is best used for goals that have an element of higher need, or those done in desperation. It involves not only appeals to the ruling powers in the Underworld, but also to the free souls of deceased human beings; and it is better if those people have died recently, and (if possible) violently somehow.

The ancient theory behind conjuring the souls of the violently slain to accomplish sorcerous goals was very simple: they died with bodily vitality and usually quickly, potentially leaving their free souls (or other aspects of their former self) closely connected to the earthly plane. There was also a belief, prominent in many places in Old Europe, that people who "died untimely", or who had died "before their time" were compelled to wander the world until their natural time arrived, before being able to move on. This left them vulnerable (or sometimes amenable) to sorcerous interactions with living human beings.

In Southern Europe, it was often the free souls of slain gladiators or professional fighters that were targeted by this spell. The work was ideally carried out in the place where they had actually died, not in the place where they were buried. It could have been used after a battle had occurred, to attempt to attract the souls of soldiers or warriors that had just been killed; such work would have been done at the site of a battlefield.

In modern times, it's more likely that (if a person is going to attempt this working in its full traditional form) one might work at the scene of an accident in which people died, or the scene of a violent crime in which someone lost their life. So long as the person didn't die of old age or an illness, the working's central metaphysical intent remains intact.

But this working can also be carried out in a graveyard or a burial ground, for such places will usually contain the bodies of people who have died in such ways. The work is *always* more potent if it is performed soon after the time of their deaths (or burials). As a last resort (which still might yield results) one can attempt this working anywhere or at any time, so long as it is done on bare earth, fully in contact with the ground. The earth itself is a massive barrow or burial-ground for all the dead, as well as an enormous system of connected places, wherein all manner of beautiful and terrible things occur. The deep system of related and overlapping forces and places, accessed through the ground, will yield the potential for an operant of this spell to gain connection to the powers that are sought.

Another variant on this work involves invoking the name of a specific person who has just recently perished through accident or violence. Even if one cannot perform a sorcerous working at the location of the death soon after they have died, or at their burial site, performing this work outdoors (and as soon as possible after their death) and calling upon their name might be efficacious. Instead of saying " O luckless ones…" in the first paragraph of the spell, it should be changed to say "O John Doe, slain (or killed) on XX day, in XX place, who wanders now in the dark unseen, upon the ghost roads or in invisible spaces yet still bound to this world…" You'd also alter the future parts of the spell that mention the dead, to include the name of the person.

This variant isn't likely to work if you are calling upon a person who died overseas or across the country that you heard about on the news. It's really only practically workable if you're somewhere reasonably near where the dead person lived or died.

Before you venture to the place where you will attempt this working (and while this operation is best done at twilight or at night, nothing stops it from being done during the day) take a piece of bread and eat a portion of it. Break the portion that remains into seven pieces and carry them with you to the location. If you prefer, you can have this "meal" at the actual place you will be doing the working; before you begin, eat your part of the bread, then break the remaining part into seven pieces.

When you have your seven pieces of bread, perform a Breaching charm and then speak this incantation over the pieces of bread:

"To the dark women of Fate, those who weave destinies, to the malign powers, to them who weave famine and jealousy, to those who died untimely deaths and those dead by woeful violence, I am sending to you this meal of bread; take this food from my hands.

Three-headed Queen of Spirits, Lady of the Night, who feeds on filth and decay, O Maiden, you key-holding Ruler of Annwn, White Phantom Queen, grim-eyed, dreadful, girt with fiery serpents, I (*say your name*) have mixed my tears and bitter groans with these leftovers from my food, so that you, O luckless ones (who are bound here in X place*) who wander now in the dark unseen, upon the ghost roads or in invisible spaces yet still bound to this world, may bring success to me, for I am beset by torments (or needs) requiring the X thing to be accomplished (*state your need briefly here.*)

You who have left the light, O you unfortunate ones, bring success to me, X (say your name) who is distressed at heart because of (*state your need briefly.*) So help me to obtain what I desire! Hasten to help me, and I will reward you with grateful offerings of wine, rich fat, and strong liquors (*you can add other potential offerings of gratitude you might be willing to make here.*)

EIOUT ABAÔTH PSAKERBA ARBATHIAÔ LALAOITH IÔSACHÔTOU ALLALETHÔ!

You as well, Great One, Queen of Spirits, Lady of Annwn, who feeds upon filth and decay:

SYNATRAKABI BAUBARABAS ENPHNOUN MORKA ERESCHIGAL NEBOUTOSOUALÊTH and send forth the Fury **ORGOGORGONIOTRIAN**, who rouses up with fire the souls of the dead, unlucky men and unlucky women, who in this place, who on this day (or night) who in this hour, give heed to me and accomplish what I desire X (*say your need here.*)

O Mistress Hekate, **PHORBA PHORBÔBAR BARÔ PHÔRPHÔR PHÔRBAI!**

O Lady of the Crossroads, O Black Bitch!"

Then throw the seven pieces of bread upon the ground in the place of your working, and depart. If you are working to harm someone, or compel them in some manner, take some dirt from the place where you have worked, and scatter it in a place where that person will have to walk, or (if you can) throw it into their house somewhere.

You should perform this rite in just the same way for three days (or nights) in a row.

* * *

If things go your way, don't forget to repay as you promised. If success or satisfaction for you does not come, you can choose to intensify this rite using the process below. Be cautious in so doing; pushing an issue with such a dark working as this exposes an operant to potential strong debts.

Return to the place of your working, and again perform the ritual of the seven pieces of bread, as written above. After you have cast the seven pieces of bread to the ground, make a pile of ashes that were created from burning flax (flax seeds will suffice) and upon that pile of ash, place a piece of dung from a black cow or some black animal. Then say:

> "King of the Underworld, Queen of Spirits in the dark below, you spirits who guide the deceased into their timeless rest, you resounding waters that separate the quick from the dead, you spirits of darkness that eat flesh, you great and forgotten powers in the depths, you, powerful Amphiaraos, and all the chthonic spirits I call! I also call you, attendants of the grave and the Underworld, you sins sunk in the ground, you dreams inside the hollows of the land, you oaths sworn on the earth and darkness, the Queen of the cold hills and the dead below them, the great abyss, and the witchery of the ghost-world. Those who escort the dead across the waters dividing, them I call upon, and the souls of men and women who wander. Come, you dark women of Fate, you who weave destinies, accomplish what I desire X (*say your desire here*)
>
> Because I am calling primal Chaos, the power before powers, the dark realm of Annwn, the awful waters that sunder the breathing world from the world of the dead, along with the waters that wash away the memories of those who have died and gone below; O Gwynnevar, Queen of spirits and dead souls, O Gwyn, King of ghosts and spirits, O you who pass

judgments upon souls, you who keep the gates and portals of Hell, open them for me quickly! Key-holder, send up to me the phantoms of the dead to serve me in this very hour, so that they might go and accomplish X (*state what you need or desire.*)"

Then take more dirt from the place of your working and use it as before, assuming you were using it in the first place.

**

Pronunciation of the Strange Words used in this invocation:

ay-oot ah-bah-oat sock-er-bah ar-bah-tee-ah-oh lah-lah-oyt ee-oh-sock-oh-too all-lah-let-oh

soon-ah-trah-kah-bee boe-bar-ah-bas in-puh-noon marka eh-ress-kee-gall neh-boot-ah-soo-ah-late … ar-gah-gar-gahn-ee-oh-tree-ahn

par-bah par-boe-bar bah-roe pour-pour pour-bay

*The statement "who are bound here in X place" is an optional line that can be used if you are in a place especially associated with the dead (like a cemetery) or in a place that was the site of a recent accidental or violent death; the place should be identified: "who are bound here in this forest" or "who are bound here where these two roads meet", etc. If you feel the power of the place strongly, or if it feels as though it should be invoked, use this line. If not, it can be left out.

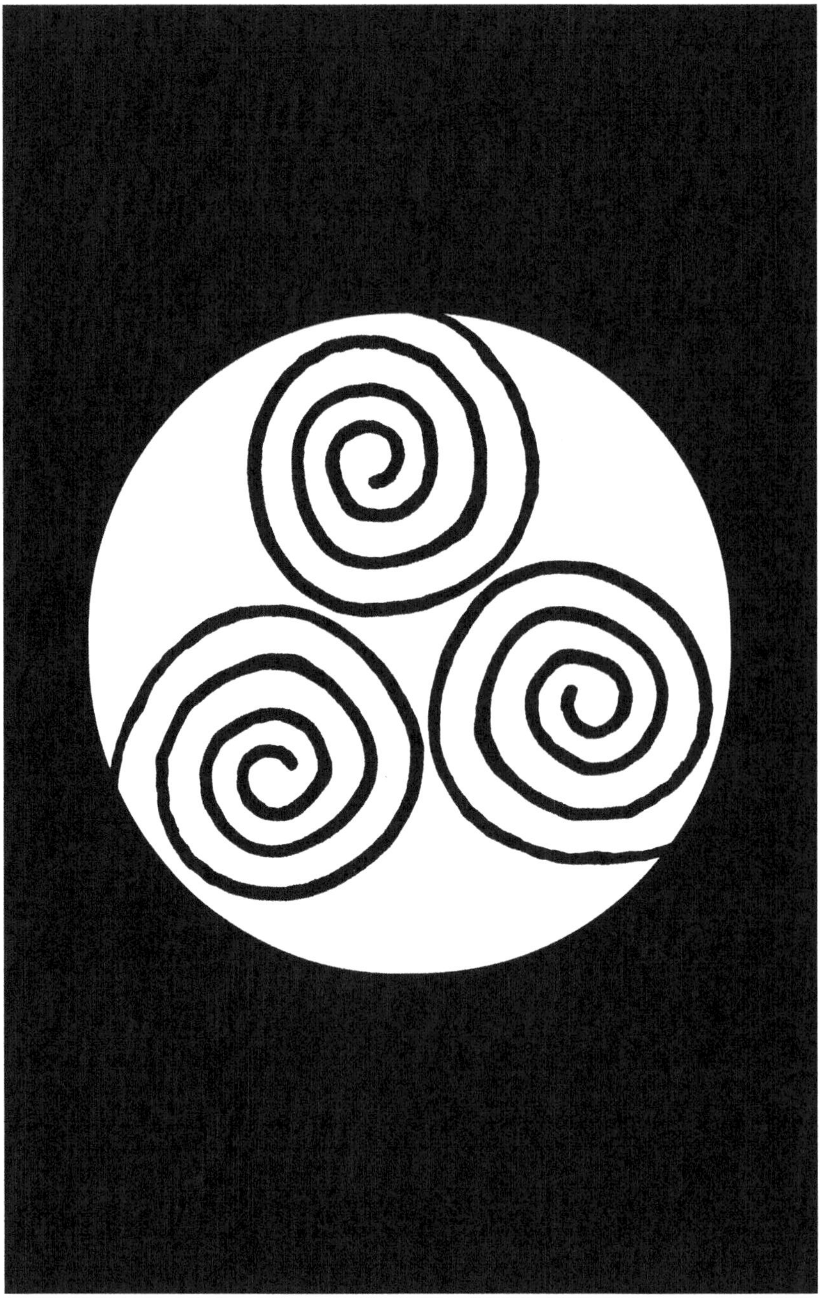

ELFHAME PRAYER

This general purpose petition to the Queen of Elfhame is especially strong for requests dealing with protection, whether from foes, wicked magic, or other dangers. Despite its traditional ancient use as a phylactery or a protective charm, it may be used for other needs that carry some element of pressing need. This petition-charm is strongest when spoken under a full moon, but can be used at any time, so long as it is night and the moon is visible to you in the sky.

Perform a Breaching charm. Then make this incantation to the moon:

"ACHTHIÔPHIPH ERESCHIGAL NEBOUGOSOUALÊTH SATHÔTH SABAÔTH SABRÔTH"

Then speak your request. If you desire, you can say the incantation three times or nine times before you make your request, to add to its power.

* * *

The Strange Words in this incantation are pronounced as so:

akh-tee-oh-peep eh-res-kee-gall neh-boo-gah-soo-ah-late sah-towt sah-bah-oat sah-brote

"akh" sounds like "ah" with a hard k ending

"towt" rhymes with "boat."

"oat" is like the "oat" in "oatmeal."

"brote" also rhymes with "boat."

ΑΝΦΑΣ

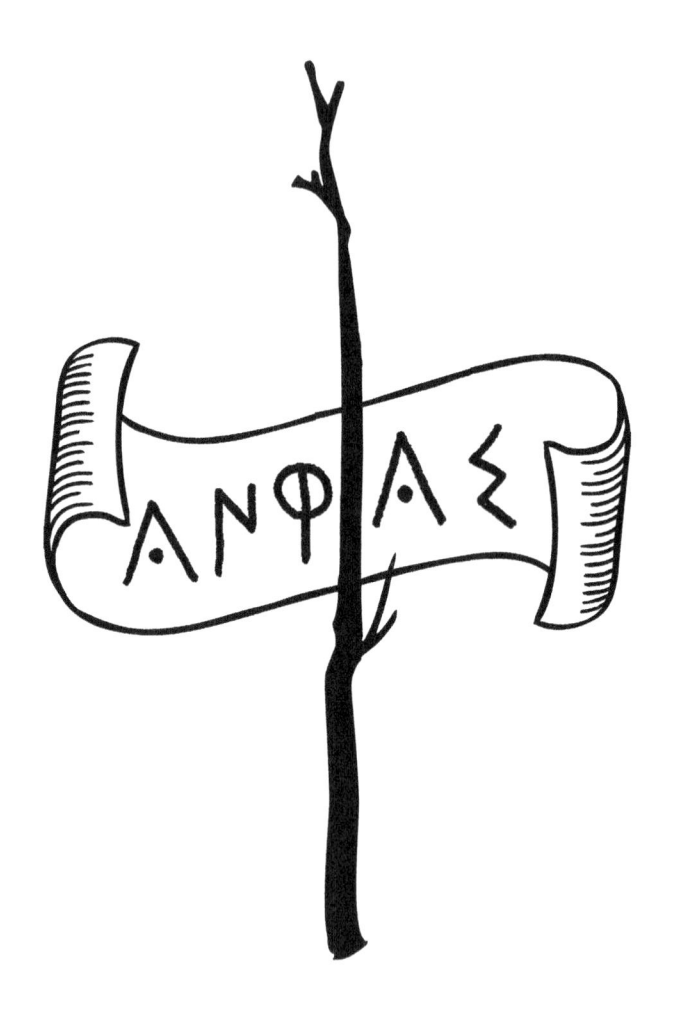

DREAM REVELATION CHARM

Take a strip of linen or some cloth, and with an ink you have made with your own hands*, write upon it the matter that you wish to obtain a dream-vision or dream revelation about. Wrap the cloth around the branch of a tree (Ash would be a good choice, but any will do) and place it to the left of your head when you lie down to go to sleep. You must have washed yourself with birch water or engaged some other purifying method before this.

Just before you lie down, say into a lit candle or lamp of art the following spell seven times:

"Gwyn, windy Lord of this world, who are yet within me,
O circle of the moon, round and square,
Master, revealer of the words of speech,
Who turns an airy course beneath the earth,
Who holds the spirit's reins and those of the sun,
Who with the light of the Strange Powers
Gives comfort to those in Annwn,
Those mortal men and women
Who have finished life and gone below;
The deadly decree of the Fates and Master of dreams
You are said to be, who giveth oracles by day and by night;
You relieve the pains of mortal creatures with your power.
Come hither O Blessed One,
Mighty One who brings visions,
With your ghostly shape and beneficent mind.
To me, an uncorrupted youth*, reveal a sign, give a vision;
Reveal within me your true skill of prophecy:

**OIOSENMIGADÔN ORTHÔ BAUBÔ NIOÊRE
KODÊRETH DOSÊRE SYRE SUROE SANKISTÊ
DÔDEKAKISTÊ AKROUROBORE KODÊRE
RINÔTON KOUMETANA ROUBITHA
NOUMILA PERPHEROU AROUÔRÊR AROUÊR"**

(You may add anything else you wish at the end, in the way of clarifying or repeating the nature of the dream-vision you are seeking, or whatever else; or you may add nothing.)

Then blow out the candle and go to sleep, with the linen or cloth-wrapped branch to the left of your head, as said before. If you have an all-night candle in a shielded receptacle, you might leave it burning all night if you wish.

You may also perform a Breaching charm before this work, which will surely add to its strength, but it is not necessary. Simply saying the words of the *Gartref chant* three times before the first time you say the spell would be a potent optional addition to the work. Those who have a difficult time remembering how many times they have said the spell can use seven stones to count the repetitions.

* * *

Pronunciation of the Strange Words used in this charm:

oy-ah-sen-mee-guh-doan ar-toe boe-boe nee-ah-ay-reh kah-day-ret dah-say-reh soor-eh soor-ah-eh sahn-kees-tay doe-deh-kah-kees-tay ahk-roo-rah-bah-reh koh-day-reh ree-noe-tahn koo-meh-tah-nah roo-bee-tuh noo-mee-lah pair-pair-oo ah-roo-oh-ray-er ah-roo-air

"doan" rhymes with the word "loan."

"toe" sounds like the English word "toe", as the toes on your feet.

"bow" sounds like the "bow" in "to take a bow before the audience"

"reh" sounds like "red" without the "d"

"sahn" sounds like the "son" in "sonic"

"ahk" sounds like "ah" but ending with a sudden "k" sound.

"noe" sounds like the English word "no."

"tahn" sounds like the "ton" in "tonic"

*The simplest way to make the ink for this charm is to take small pieces of dry wood or charcoal and burn them to ash. Then reduce the ash to a very fine powder and mix in an equal part of water, stirring very well. Add a drop of vinegar to it as you stir, if you can. This ink can be stored in a jar with a tight-fitting lid, which should be kept in a dark place.

*The "uncorrupted youth" is a poetic reference to the timeless and ageless free soul within a person, not a reference to a person's chronological age.

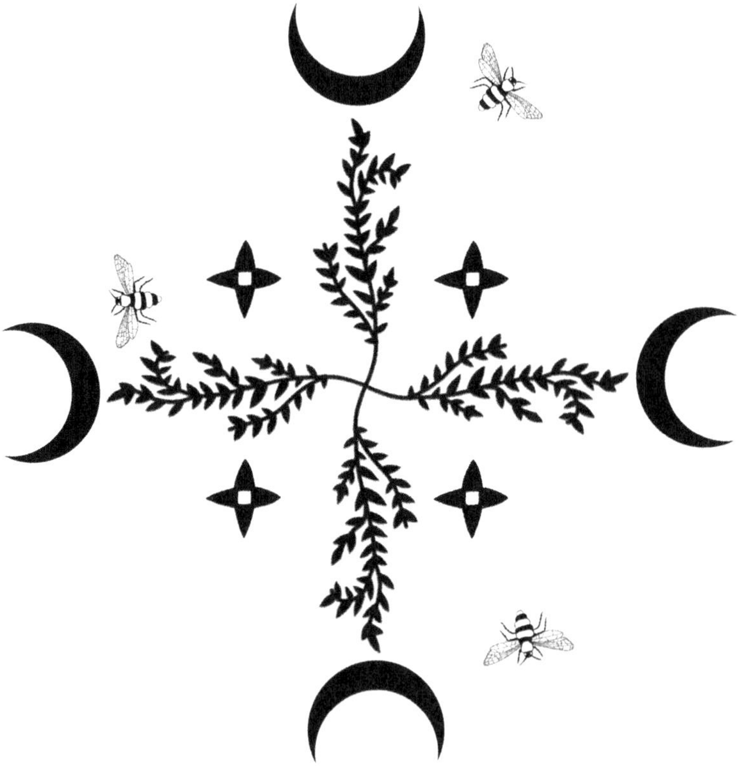

APPEAL TO THE WORT WEIRD

The following charm is an alternate Herb Swaying Charm, drawing upon two "plant picking" charms given in the ancient source materials. The Semoferas Words used in the Herb Swaying Charm can be spoken before this appeal-invocation is made; they have been inserted into the spell itself for convenience. This charm should be performed in the same way and with the same understandings as the Herb Swaying Charm. You do not have to perform a Breaching charm before utilizing this working, but it never hinders a working if you do.

Traditionally, you should do this work before sunrise, and you must be purified by some traditional means. Give a small gift of whole cream, honey, or a drop of your blood for what you take. If for some reason you harvest the entire plant- taking it out of the ground by its roots- you must repay the earth with a larger measure of honey, whole cream, and (if possible) seven seeds or groats of barley or wheat. If the uprooted plant was potted, you must still make this repayment to the ground outside.

(Lyaham, Lyalgama, Lyafar, Vyalurab, Lelara, Lebaron, Laasalilus)

"You were sown by the virile Lord of the World,
You were conceived by the Lady of the Good Earth,
You were given birth and nourished by the rains,
You were given growth by the power of the ground,
The light from above, and the dew of the air.

You are the dew of all the sacred powers:
You are the eye of glory, the light of the moon,
The strength of the Lord of the Underworld,
The beauty of the green land.

You are the soul of the Wandering One
Who moves everywhere upon the earth;
Your roots come from the depths,
But your powers are in the heart of the Master of Sorcery,
And the Lady who gives nourishment to all.

Your flowers are the eyes of spirits unseen,
Your seed is the seed of the Lord of Life.
I take a portion of you, (name of plant)
With my five-fingered hand.
I, (say your name)
Am taking this portion of you for my own
So that it may work for me, for a certain purpose.

In the name of the King of Spirits and his Queen,
In the names of the holy Earth and Sky,
I adjure you to help me and aid me in my task.
Be kind, and the Good Earth will flow with water for you,
And my gratitude will flow just the same.

**MOUTHABAR NACH BARNACHÔCHA BRAEÔ
MENDA LAUBRAASSE PHASPHA BENDEÔ**

Fulfill for me this perfect charm."

* * *

Pronunciation of the Strange Words used in this invocation:

moo-tah-bar nock barn-ah-koh-kah brah-eh-oh
men-dah loe-brah-oss-eh pahs-pah ben-deh-oh

ABOUT THE AUTHOR

Robin Artisson is the author of *"An Carow Gwyn: Sorcery and the Ancient Fayerie Faith"* and twelve other works on the topics of folklore, sorcery, spiritual ecology, witchcraft, and ancient esoteric beliefs and practices. He lives on the coast of Maine, but can often be found in its wooded interior, climbing mountains or making offerings to the spirits that indwell its landscape.

Printed in Great Britain
by Amazon